Make Your Own Art

Eco-Crafts

Sally Henry and Trevor Cook

1

PowerKiDS
press.

New York

Published in 2011 by The Rosen Publishing Group, Inc.
29 East 21st Street, New York, NY 10010

Text and design: Sally Henry and Trevor Cook
Editor: Joe Harris
U.S. editor: Kara Murray
Photography: Sally Henry and Trevor Cook

Library of Congress Cataloging-in-Publication Data

Henry, Sally.
Eco crafts / by Sally Henry and Trevor Cook.
    p. cm. — (Make your own art)
Includes index.
ISBN 978-1-4488-1582-1 (library binding) — ISBN 978-1-4488-1611-8 (pbk.) —
ISBN 978-1-4488-1612-5 (6-pack)
1. Nature craft. I. Cook, Trevor, 1948- II. Title.
TT157.H43 2011
745.5—dc22
                        2010027715

Printed in the United States

SL001620US

CPSIA Compliance Information: Batch #WA11PK: For Further Information contact Rosen Publishing, New York, New York at 1-800-237-9932

Contents

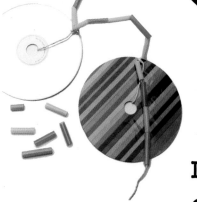

Introduction

There are two kinds of projects in this book. The first kind of project gives suggestions about how you can support and protect wildlife in your local area. The second kind is about reusing things. By reusing and recycling, you can reduce your impact on the environment.

household waste

Paper

One of the materials we'll be using is **waste paper**. Every day people throw huge amounts of this away, but it's a tremendous resource for the artist. Look out for printed paper, such as newspapers and magazines, advertising flyers, and packaging. All are great sources of pictures and color. The gift boxes on pages 24–25 are decorated with pictures on paper that would usually be thrown away.

paper

You'll need colored **tissue paper** for some projects. You can buy this from craft stores, or rescue it from packaging.

tissue paper

Glass

glass

The **jars** we use in the glow jars project on pages 8–9 used to be full of food. Before using jars in a craft project, make sure that the food has all been used up, and clean them thoroughly.

Plastics

Packaging materials such as plastic cases and bubble wrap are a problem for recycling, but great for making models. The alligator on pages 18–19 is an example of seeing simple shapes in a new way.

plastics

Modeling clay

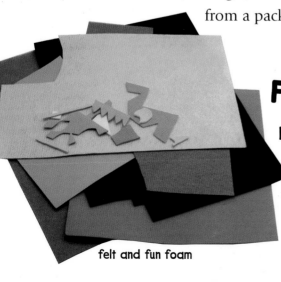

We also use **modeling clay** that hardens by drying in the air, or by heating in an oven. If you want to use clay that dries in an oven, be sure to follow the manufacturer's directions for the correct time and temperature to use. Use oven-safe dishes to hold your models and allow plenty of time for cooling.

modeling clay

card stock and cardboard

Card stock and cardboard

Things made from **card stock** or **cardboard** often form the starting point for our projects. Card stock is bendable, like thick paper. The juice cartons we use to make the cat bookends on pages 14–15 are made from a waxy type of card stock that is hard to recycle, but is perfect for re-use. Cardboard is thicker, stronger, and harder, and is often made of layers of card stock. We cut some from a packing case to make the spine of the alligator on pages 18–19.

Felt and fun foam

Felt is a material made of matted wool and is dyed bright colors. It is easy to cut with **scissors** and gives a really neat edge. **Fun foam** (sometimes called EVA) is a more modern material, but is safe, non-toxic, and washable. It is also easy to cut with scissors and comes in bright colors. It's soft and bendable but sticks well with **rubber cement** (see page 6).

felt and fun foam

Paints and crayons

Any water-based **paint** can be used for painting your projects. A small amount of bright color goes a long way. Try to paint on a white background. It makes colors look brighter.

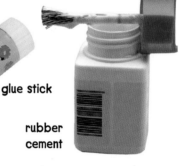
wax crayons

Wax crayons are necessary for the batik paper on pages 26–27.

Glue

We've used mostly a glue called **white glue** to make our projects. It's white, but becomes clear when it's dry.

water-based paints

To stick paper to paper or paper to card stock, we sometimes use a **glue stick**. It's quick and clean, but not really as lasting as white glue.

glue stick

rubber cement

Rubber cement is flexible and water-based. It's good for sticking soft materials like cloth, felt, or fun foam.

white glue

Natural materials

stones

We've used **stones** for the paperweight family on pages 28–29, and flowers for the pressed flowers and bookmarks projects on pages 20–21 and 22–23. Stones will need to be washed before you use them. Make sure that you have permission from whoever owns the garden before you start picking flowers.

Tools

We always need **scissors** for whatever we're making. Choose a pair with rounded ends because they're safer!

scissors

Some things are hard to cut out with scissors and are much easier with a **craft knife**, such as the holes in the bird feeder. Always get an adult to help you with knives as they can be dangerous if used incorrectly!

Bending wire is a lot easier with a pair of **pliers**. You'll need some if you make the bird feeder and the CD mobile!

A **paper punch** cuts neat holes and makes little round shapes at the same time. We use a punch for the bookmarks on pages 22–23.

craft knife

pliers

It's important to have a good **ruler** for such projects as the gift box on pages 24–25.

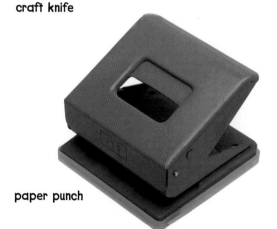

paper punch

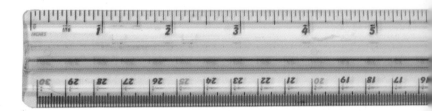

ruler

7

Clean and safe

When you're making your projects, you need **somewhere to work** that's easy to clean. Glue is hard to get off fur and fabrics, so avoid carpets, curtains, and pets. A kitchen is an ideal place, but be sure to ask first. Sometimes there's other work being done there! Put sheets of newspaper down to protect work surfaces. Also, before you start, it's a good idea to prepare somewhere to put things while they dry.

Glow Jars

Transform empty jelly jars into pretty, glowing decorations!

30 MINUTES

5 MINUTES

You will need:

- *Two clean, glass jelly jars*
- *Black paper • Colored tissue paper*
- *White glue • Scissors*
- *Marker pen • Tealight candles*
- *Matches (you'll need an adult to supervise while you're using these)*

What to do...

These attractive decorations would brighten up anyone's day! We decided to decorate them with winter trees, but you can create your own cutouts for any occasion. The finished glow jars can be used as lanterns or as table decorations. This project requires few materials, but produces really great results.

Coat the outside of a jar with white glue and wrap yellow tissue paper around it.

Cut strips of spiky grass from green tissue and stick them around the base of the jar.

Cut red and orange circles in tissue paper and stick them all around the top half of the jar.

Cut two trees out of black paper. Stick them on the front and the back of the jar.

Fold over 4 layers of tissue to make a strong strip.

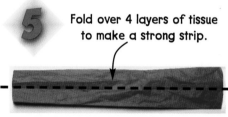

Fold and glue some red tissue to make a narrow handle. Glue the handle to the top of the jar.

Glue well to make a safe handle.

Glue a folded strip of red tissue around the top of the jar, and cover the ends of the handle.

tealight candle inside the jelly jar

Place a tealight candle inside the jar. Ask an adult to light it. Be careful. The jars may get hot!

Bird Feeder

Attract wild birds into your garden with this fun bird feeder.

30 MINUTES   **2 MINUTES**

You will need:

- *Large plastic bottle*
- *Piece of dowel .4 by 10 inches (10 x 260 mm)*
- *White glue • Scissors*
- *String or garden wire*
- *Craft knife • Pieces of fun foam*
- *Wild bird food • Pieces of fruit*
- *White plastic bag • Hole punch*

What to do...

A plastic bottle is a perfect container for bird food. It keeps the food clean and dry. It's easy to hang it up somewhere that's safe for birds to perch and feed. You can look up on the Internet what the best food is for the birds in your area.

1

Leave the lid on.

Make sure your bottle is clean and dry. Remove any labels.

2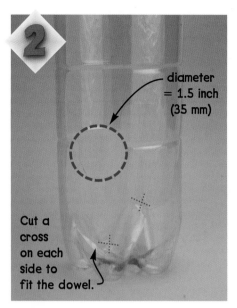

diameter = 1.5 inch (35 mm)

Cut a cross on each side to fit the dowel.

Get an adult to help you cut a hole for the birds to feed, and two small crosses for the perch.

3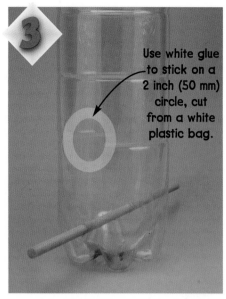

Use white glue to stick on a 2 inch (50 mm) circle, cut from a white plastic bag.

Push the dowel through the crosses to make a perch and stick on the white plastic circle.

4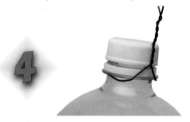

Tie a length of string or garden wire to the neck of the bottle.

5

Fill the feeder up to the holes with wild bird food.

Put the birds on either side of the hole.

6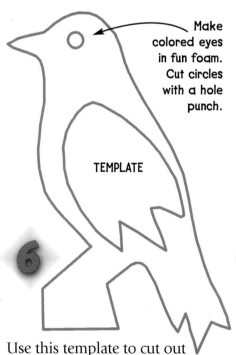

Make colored eyes in fun foam. Cut circles with a hole punch.

TEMPLATE

Use this template to cut out two birds in fun foam. Stick them on the bottle with white glue.

7 Hang the bottle from a high branch. You can tie some leaves around the top part of the bottle to shade it. Don't worry, the birds will still find the food!

Give your garden birds a special treat with this **fruit necklace**. Cut up pieces of fruit and thread them on a piece of string. Hang it up in the garden and watch the fruit disappear!

Build a Bug Box

This little house will encourage the insects that are good for your garden. You'll need a grown-up's help to make it.

| 2 HOURS | 5 MINUTES |

You will need:

- *Four pieces of untreated wood, about 4 by 2.5 by .75 inch (110 x 65 x 20 mm)*
- *One piece of untreated wood for the back of the box, about 4 by 7 inches (110 x 170 mm)*
- *Hollow canes, bamboo, or something similar*
- *Small wooden branch*
- *1.5 inch (35mm) nails*
- *Hammer • Drill • Wood drill bit*
- *Sharp pointed screw and screwdriver to fit it*
- *Help from an adult with a saw*

What to do...

Give nature a helping hand in your garden by providing a perfect home for useful insects such as bees, spiders, and tiny ladybugs. Use old scrap timber (not treated with wood preserver or paint), old bamboo canes, and fallen branches.

This piece of old floorboard and these bamboo sticks have been in a corner of the garden for a while.

Get an adult to help you cut the plank into pieces.

Nail the pieces together like this.

Put the back on with more nails.

Cut another piece of wood to fit on the back. Make it 1 inch (25 mm) higher than the box, and make a hole in the middle.

Put in as many pieces as will fit.

Cut pieces of bamboo and branch the same depth as the box. Drill holes in the ends of the pieces of branch.

A sharp screw makes it easy to fix to a fence post or even a tree.

It's ready. Let's find a place for it in the garden!

Cat Bookends

You can make these handy bookends from juice boxes. They're perfect for keeping your books neat and they make a great present.

60 MINUTES

10 MINUTES

You will need:

- *Two empty juice cartons*
- *White glue • Black permanent marker pen*
- *Colored tissue paper • Used plain white paper*
- *Thick cardboard • Ruler • Tracing paper*
- *Paints • Brushes • Scissors • Varnish*
- *Dry sand • Tape*

What to do...

Find two empty juice cartons that are the same size. Wash them out with water and make sure they're not sticky. Bookends need to be heavy, so use sand to weight them down. We're going to cover everything in plain white paper. The back of used printer paper is fine to use.

Paint both sides of the tail and the back of the ears.

Use a permanent black marker pen to draw the lines.

1 Copy the templates of the cat and the tail onto sturdy white paper, then paint them. Cut around both shapes and glue them on thick cardboard with a glue stick.

2 Cut around the shapes on the cardboard with scissors. Glue plain white paper to the other side of the card and trim neatly. Paint the tail and the ears of the cat. These will show above the box.

4 Fill the carton with dry sand. Fold the flap over to close the box and secure it with tape. Repeat this with the other carton. Cover the cartons with white paper torn into small pieces and white glue. Paint the cartons to match your cat. Glue the cardboard parts to the cartons and allow them to dry completely before use.

3 Measure 4 inches (100 mm) on your carton. Draw a line around the carton. Cut along the two short sides and the front. Make a flap from the back panel to fold down and close the top of the box.

4 inches (100 mm)

CD Mobile

Here's a wildlife-friendly way of scaring birds away from fruit or vegetables in your garden!

10
MINUTES

1
MINUTE

You will need:

- Old CDs or DVDs
- String • Wire coat hanger
- Bright wrapping paper
- Colored drinking straws
- Pliers • Scissors • White glue
- Paint and brushes

What to do...

Rescue those unwanted CDs and DVDs from the trash and put them to good use.

Sometimes we need to keep birds off our fruit and vegetable gardens. These bright, shiny disks will do the job as they flash and clatter in the wind!

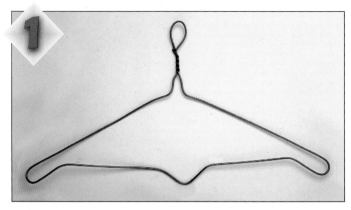

Open the scissors a little, and push them from one end to the other, making a long cut.

Make the coat hanger hook into a loop and bend the bottom part to stop the string from slipping.

Cut down the sides of some drinking straws, then cut them into .8 inch (20 mm) beads.

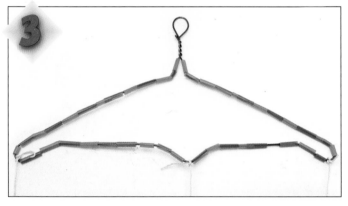

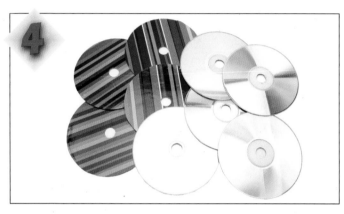

17

Push pieces of straw onto the coat hanger. Then tie three strings to the hanger.

Paint the label side of your old disks with bright colors, or glue on some patterned paper.

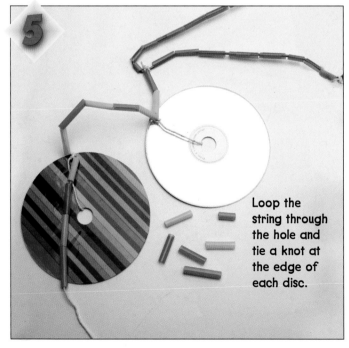

Loop the string through the hole and tie a knot at the edge of each disc.

Thread more straw beads onto the strings, and tie on the disks every 6 inches (150 mm).

When you've finished three strings of disks, your mobile is finished. Let's find somewhere to hang it up!

Little Alligator

Reuse some plastic bottles to make a tough little monster!

You will need:

- *Two plastic bottles*
- *White glue • Bubble wrap*
- *Colored tissue paper*
- *Scissors • Tape • Newspaper*
- *White card stock • Black paper*
- *Fun foam or colored felt*
- *Craft knife • Googly eyes*
- *Four wine corks • Cardboard*

What to do...

After you've finished a drink, keep the bottle! You can turn something you generally throw away into a little monster that you can use as a toy or room decoration.

45
MINUTES

5
MINUTES

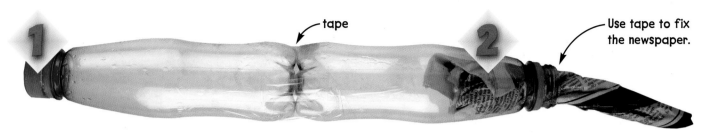

1

tape

Join two empty plastic bottles of the same size together with tape. Put a cap on one of the bottles.

2

Use tape to fix the newspaper.

Make a tail with rolled newspaper. Push it into the neck of the bottle.

3

Ask an adult to help you cut four corks to the same length, 1 inch (25 mm), for legs. Glue the legs to the body with tissue paper soaked in white glue.

Cut the corks at a 45°angle.

4

Roll up pieces of newspaper to make eyes and nostrils. Glue them in place with white glue and tissue paper.

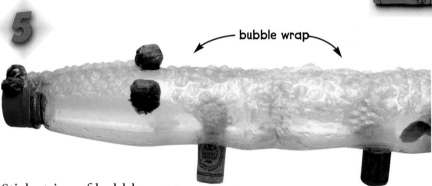

5

bubble wrap

Stick strips of bubble wrap on the back and the snout with tape.

6

Build up several layers of tissue.

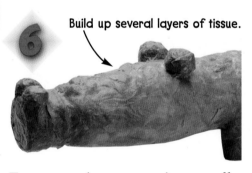

Tear green tissue paper into small pieces and stick them all over the bottles with white glue.

7

Cut 16 spines from cardboard. Cover with green tissue paper and white glue. Glue the spines along the center of the back with white glue. Cut four pads (see template) from fun foam and stick one to the base of each leg.

PAD TEMPLATE
Cut 4 pieces.

8

Cut nostrils from fun foam.

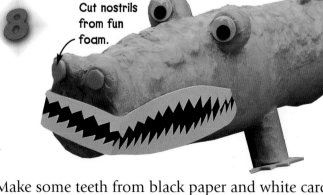

Make some teeth from black paper and white card stock and stick them on with white glue. Add some googly eyes and your alligator is finished!

Pressed Flowers

The old-fashioned pastime of pressing flowers can be really fun. You can make wonderful greetings cards with just a little patience!

30 MINUTES **5 MINUTES**

PLUS ABOUT **1** WEEK OF PRESSING!

You will need:

- *Freshly picked flowers and leaves*
- *Thin card stock • Envelopes*
- *Colored markers*
- *Paper towels*
- *Several heavy books for weights*
- *White glue • Brush • Scissors*
- *Old newspapers*

What to do...

Keep your flowers standing in water until you are ready to press them.

Ask an adult if you can pick some garden flowers. Choose the flowers you want to press. Trim off any bushy leaves and shorten the stems.

Put a paper towel on a folded newspaper. Lay the flowers and some leaves on the towel. Cover with another piece of paper towel.

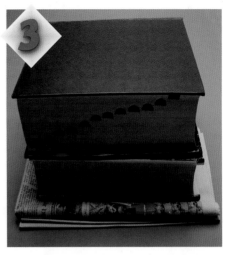

Put a second newspaper on top of the paper towel and cover with heavy books. Leave for at least a week!

Draw a fine colored line on the front of the card.

Prepare some white cards, by cutting and folding them to fit your envelopes. Our cards are 6 by 4 inches (150 x 100 mm). Draw a colored line on the front of the card .5 inch (12 mm) inside the edge.

Note: You need to leave flowers pressing under the books for as long as possible. Colors may get paler after pressing.

Work on a flat surface and try to be very neat. Think about how you are going to arrange your flowers. You can start by sticking the largest one in the middle of the card with white glue. Add the smaller flowers to make a pretty group.

Allow the glue to dry from time to time so that the flowers don't move while you are working. Finally, stick on the leaves, covering the stems, to form a basket holding the flowers. Allow everything to dry, then write your message in the card.

Eco Bookmarks

It's easier than you might think to make your own recycled paper. You can turn the paper into a pretty and practical gift by mounting it on card as a bookmark.

45
MINUTES

10
MINUTES

You will need:

- *Scraps of white and colored paper*
- *Net curtain or muslin*
- *Dried flowers • Large spoon*
- *Old picture frame (without glass or picture) • Staple gun • Glue stick*
- *Electric blender • Hot (not boiling) water • Large tray • Rolling pin*
- *Old newspapers • Black paper*
- *Paper punch • Gift ribbon*

What to do

It's fun to recycle your scrap paper! Collect several sheets of used white paper and as many color scraps as you can. Tear the paper into small pieces. You need about two handfuls. Ask an adult to help you with using the blender.

1

Wash out the blender thoroughly after use.

Put some torn paper into the blender. Half-fill the blender with hot tap water. Put the lid on and blend for 30 seconds.

2

Staple all round on the sides.

Turn the frame over to put the pulp mixture in.

Stretch the old net curtain or muslin tight over the picture frame. Staple around the edge.

3

Put the frame over a tray. Spoon the wet paper mixture onto the muslin.

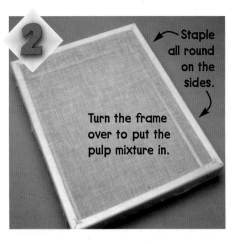

4

Spread the mixture evenly with the spoon. Shake the tray from side to side to get rid of the water and even out the pulp. Put some pressed flowers on top of the pulp.

5

Put the tray on a pad of old newspaper. Use another pad of newspaper to soak up the water from the top of the pulp. Replace the newspaper until the pulp is just damp.

6

Turn the tray over onto dry newspaper. Tap the frame gently to release the pulp into the tray.

23

7

Cover the pulp with newspaper and roll it with a rolling pin. Repeat with more dry paper.

8

Let your recycled sheet dry in the air. It will get lighter in color when fully dried.

9

To make a bookmark, cut your paper into strips, stick it to black card stock with a glue stick, and tie on a thin ribbon.

Gift Boxes

Make a collage gift box from an old cereal box and some glue!

45 MINUTES

5 MINUTES

You will need:

- *Piece of card stock, 9.5 by 7.5 inches (240 x 190 mm) – an old cereal box is fine*
- *Collage paper, such as pictures cut from magazines or used gift wrapping*
- *Scissors • Used up ballpoint or rollerball pen*
- *White glue • Ribbon*

What to do...

This is a simple box that you can use to wrap that special little gift. Reuse some card stock cut from a cereal box. Add some glue and some printed paper. We've used pictures of pets from magazines and old stamps, but you can use comics, drawings, photographs, or anything on paper!

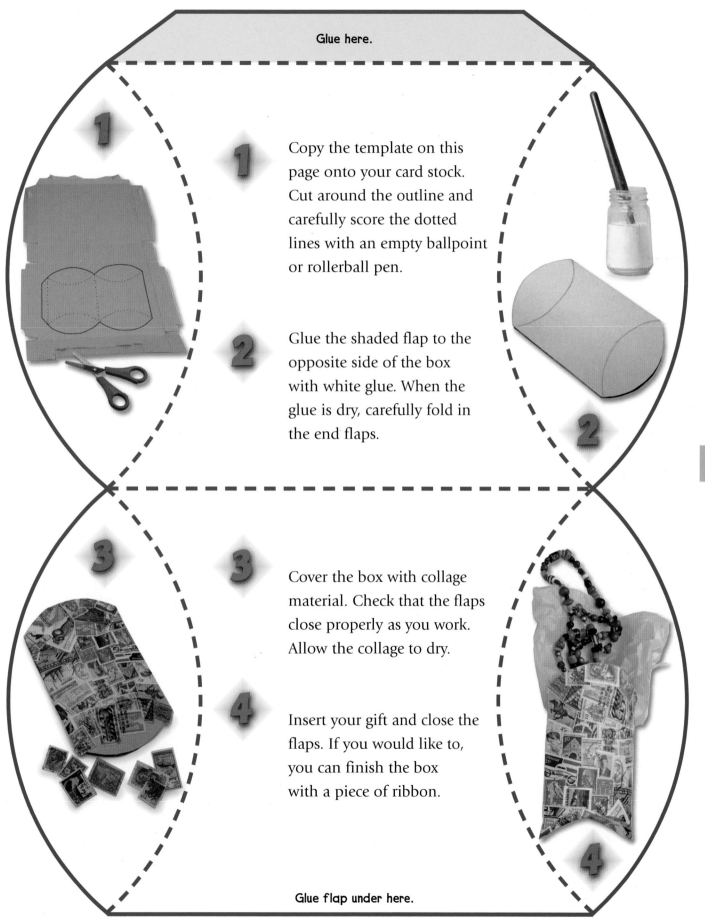

Glue here.

1 Copy the template on this page onto your card stock. Cut around the outline and carefully score the dotted lines with an empty ballpoint or rollerball pen.

2 Glue the shaded flap to the opposite side of the box with white glue. When the glue is dry, carefully fold in the end flaps.

3 Cover the box with collage material. Check that the flaps close properly as you work. Allow the collage to dry.

4 Insert your gift and close the flaps. If you would like to, you can finish the box with a piece of ribbon.

Glue flap under here.

Batik Paper

This decorative paper is easy and fun to make.

30 MINUTES

2 MINUTES

You will need:

- *Wax crayons (broken and small pieces will do)* • *Pencil*
- *Two sheets of white paper* • *Old newspapers* • *Brush*
- *Black water-based paint* • *Electric iron* • *Paper towel*

What to do...

Use scrap paper and old wax crayons to create this beautiful piece of work.

3 Crumple your paper into a tight ball, but don't throw it away! Unfold it, flatten it out, and lay it on some dry newspaper. Ask an adult to turn on an electric iron for you (medium setting, non-steam), to get ready for step 5.

1 Draw an interesting pattern in pencil. Color it in with bright wax crayons.

2 Apply the crayons thickly. Don't leave any white paper showing!

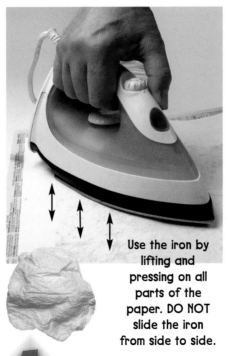

Use the iron by lifting and pressing on all parts of the paper. DO NOT slide the iron from side to side.

4 Paint all over the paper with black water-based paint. Don't worry if the wax resists it. Allow the paint to soak into the paper for a few minutes.

5 Mop up any excess liquid with a paper towel. Cover your work with some writing paper. Ask an adult to apply a warm, unplugged iron.

6 Let the iron cool, then put it away safely. Peel off the top sheet of paper to see your brilliant batik. Pin it up on the wall to look at from a distance. Doesn't it look great?

Stone Family Rock Band

These paperweights will brighten up the dullest of desks!

3 HOURS

10 MINUTES

You will need:

- Stones from the beach or garden
- Colored modeling clay that hardens when put in an oven • Felt or fun foam • Aluminum foil
- Card stock • Small plastic container
- Garden wire • Cocktail sticks • Barbecue skewers
- White glue • Sandpaper • Clear tape
- Scissors • Pliers • Button • Black marker

What to do...

This project is about re-using something natural and "ordinary" by turning it into an entertaining piece of art. Find stones around 3 inches (75 mm) across that are not exactly regular in shape. Odd lumps and bumps will add character to your musicians!

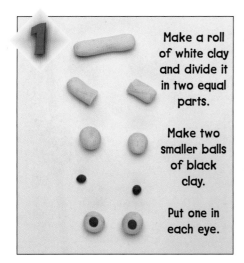

Make a roll of white clay and divide it in two equal parts.

Make two smaller balls of black clay.

Put one in each eye.

Roll clay into balls for eyes.

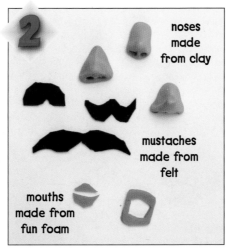

noses made from clay

mustaches made from felt

mouths made from fun foam

Make different noses, mouths, and mustaches.

Shape the feet from rolls of clay.

Press down on the feet to fit them to the shape of the stone.

Make fat rolls of modeling clay for the feet.

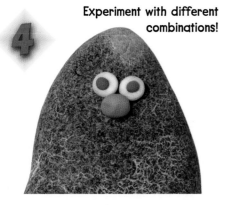

Experiment with different combinations!

Follow the instructions on the packet to harden the clay features. Glue them on with white glue.

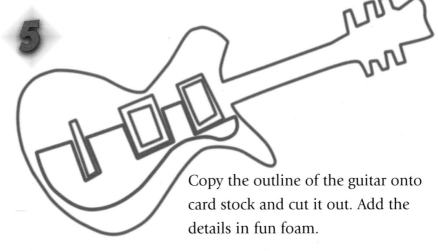

Copy the outline of the guitar onto card stock and cut it out. Add the details in fun foam.

29

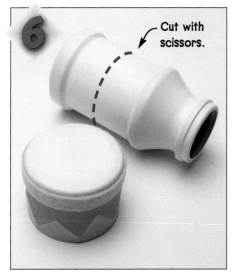

Cut with scissors.

The drum is made from half of a small, plastic spice container. Decorate with colored paper.

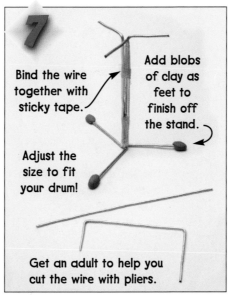

Bind the wire together with sticky tape.

Add blobs of clay as feet to finish off the stand.

Adjust the size to fit your drum!

Get an adult to help you cut the wire with pliers.

Make the drum stand from three pieces of garden wire that are bent and stuck together with tape.

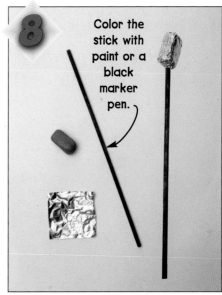

Color the stick with paint or a black marker pen.

Make a microphone from a piece of clay, wire, some foil, and a barbecue skewer.

9

Flatten a ball of clay to make the palm.

Cut finger and thumb from thin rolls of clay.

Press the parts together.

Make the hands from different parts like this.

10

Fit the guitarist's hands around the guitar.

The singer has just one hand around the microphone stand.

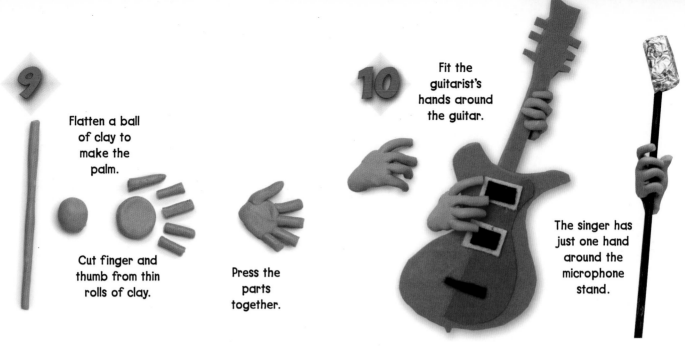

Shape the hands for each performer before hardening the clay. Put only the clay in the oven.

11

Blunt the points with fine sandpaper.

The drummer's sticks are made from halves of cocktail sticks.

12

Fix the band members' hands to their sides with white glue.

13

This guitarist has a bandana made from modeling clay. You can also make one from felt or fun foam!

Our drummer has half-closed eyes. Make eyelids from thin clay shapes.

Our singer has a fun foam flower in her hair, and thick, black felt eyebrows.

A button and some aluminum foil make a great base for the mic stand. →

Here's the band. They're ready to perform!

Glossary

aluminum foil   (uh-LOO-muh-num FOYL) A silver-colored wrapping material, used for cooking.

bandana   (ban-DA-nah) A colorful cloth worn on the neck or head.

batik   (buh-TEEK) A method of decoration using patterns drawn in wax.

blender   (BLEND-ur) An electrical device usually used to mix soft food and liquids.

carton   (KAR-tun) A cardboard box used for storage.

collage   (kuh-LAWJ) A work of art made by fixing a group of materials on a single surface.

combinations   (kahm-buh-NAY-shunz) Ways of grouping objects together.

diameter   (dy-A-meh-ter) The measurement across the center of a round object.

dowel   (DOW-ul) A round wooden peg, which fits into drilled holes, usually used to connect two pieces of wood. (Sold as a long stick of wood.)

greeting   (GREE-ting) A friendly message given on first meeting someone.

microphone stand   (MY-kroh-fohn STAND) A metal rod that holds a microphone.

nostrils   (NOS-trulz) The openings to the nose.

panel   (PA-nul) A thin, flat piece of wood or other stiff material.

paperweight   (PAY-pur-wayt) A small, heavy object used to keep office papers from blowing away.

performer   (per-FORM-ur) A person who sings, dances, or plays an instrument in public.

template   (TEM-plut) An exact version of something that makes it easy to make many copies.

Index

Web Sites

Due to the changing nature of Internet links, PowerKids Press has developed an online list of Web sites related to the subject of this book. This site is updated regularly. Please use this link to access the list:
www.powerkidslinks.com/myoa/eco/